Contents

W9-AAF-215

ReadingWise

Comprehension Strategies That Work

2

Series Consultant

Diane J. Sawyer, Ph.D.
Murfree Professor of Dyslexic Studies
Middle Tennessee State University

ReadingWise 2: Comprehension Strategies That Work
ISBN 1-56420-326-3
Copyright © 2003 New Readers Press
New Readers Press
U.S. Publishing Division of Laubach Literacy
1320 Jamesville Avenue, Syracuse, New York 13210

Printed in the United States of America
9 8 7 6 5 4 3 2 1

All proceeds from the sale of New Readers Press materials
support literacy programs in the United States and worldwide.

Developer: Kraft & Kraft, New York, NY
Series Editor: Judi Lauber
Production Director: Heather Witt
Designer: Shelagh Clancy
Illustrations: Carolyn Boehmer, Matt Terry, Linda Tiff
Production Specialist: Alexander Jones
Cover Design: Kimbrly Koennecke

To the Student

Welcome to *ReadingWise 2*.

This book will help you understand more of what you read.

Good readers think when they read. This book is about the thinking skills they use.

Life has already taught you many thinking skills. This book will show you how to use them for reading.

ReadingWise 2 has 31 lessons. Each lesson builds one skill and has four parts:

- This Is the Idea tells what skill you will learn.
- Take a Closer Look shows how to use the skill.
- Try It helps you use the skill.
- Use It lets you use the skill on your own.

Adults need to read many things every day. This book includes

- labels
- ads
- rules and directions
- charts
- menus
- news and sports reports
- magazine articles
- letters to the editor
- voting information
- and more things

When you read these things in *ReadingWise*, you practice thinking skills. And the skills help you become a better reader.

Using Word Parts

◆ *Understanding Prefixes and Suffixes*

A prefix is a word part. So is a suffix. A prefix is added at the front of a word. A suffix is added at the end of a word. These word parts change a word's meaning.

This Is the Idea

Read these words. Notice the prefix *re-* at the start of each one.

remake	replay	rerun	rework
recount	refit	relight	relive
reseal	repaint	rethink	retrain
review	rebuild	refill	rename

You know the word *make*. The prefix *re-* means "again." Now you know the word *remake*. It means "make again." Sometimes, film studios will remake a classic movie.

Take a Closer Look

Read these words. Notice the suffix *-er* at the end of each one.

helper	player	worker	backer
catcher	farmer	reader	golfer
painter	singer	talker	trainer
cleaner	banker	camper	waiter

A prefix

• *re-* can mean "again"

A suffix

• *-er* can mean "a person who does this"

Circle your answers.

1. Which word names someone who plays?
   Hint: Look for *play* in both words.
   a. painter   b. singer   c. player

2. Which word names someone who cleans?
   a. farmer   b. cleaner   c. golfer

3. Which word names someone who talks?
   a. painter   b. camper   c. talker

4. Which word names someone who sings?
   a. singer   b. backer   c. catcher

Try It

Circle your answers.

1. Which word means *read again?*
   a. reread   b. reader

2. Which word names someone who paints?
   a. repaint   b. painter

3. Which word means *wind again?*
   a. rewind   b. winder

4. Which word names someone who works?
   a. rework   b. worker

5. Which word means *train again?*
   a. retrain   b. trainer

Use It

Read this TV review. Look for words with *re-* and *-er*.

NEW SHOWS FOR THE FALL SEASON

We've had one rerun after another all summer. Now it's fall, and the new shows will begin. "My Song" is about a singer looking for her big break. "Dan's Ducks" is about a farmer and his helper. "Dan's Ducks" is supposed to be funny. Believe me, reader, it's not funny. The network has to find someone to rewrite the jokes. If they don't, "Dan's Ducks" will be this season's turkey.

Circle your answers.

1. What shows were on in the summer?
   a. old shows that ran again   b. new shows

2. Which show is about someone who sings?
   a. "My Song"   b. "Dan's Ducks"

3. Which of these is in "Dan's Ducks"?
   a. someone who reads   b. someone who farms

4. Who else is in "Dan's Ducks"?
   a. someone who runs   b. someone who helps

5. What does the network have to find someone to do?
   a. read the jokes again   b. write the jokes again

Collecting Useful Words

Look for new words that you can use. Write new words on cards. On each card, write a note that will help you learn the word.

This Is the Idea

As you read this rental ad, look for useful new words.

Room for Rent

I have a room for rent in my home. It is a large, bright room, and it is furnished. The tenant will have a private bath and share the kitchen. The house is quiet, and the rent is reasonable. I don't allow pets. Please phone Nabeel at 555-6343, after 7:00 any weekday evening.

Keep some small cards and a pen with you all the time. Let's say that the words printed in blue ink are new to you. Write each one on a card. Ask a friend how to read the words and what they mean. On each card, write a note to help you learn the word.

Take a Closer Look

Look at these word cards and read the notes on them.

Look for new words
- on signs
- in ads
- on boxes and cans
- in the news

private	tenant	reasonable
just yours	renter	fair

Draw lines to match the words and the notes. ***Hints:*** First find the word on a card. Then look at the note. Finally, find the note below.

1. private   a. fair

2. reasonable   b. just yours

3. tenant   c. renter

Try It

Here are six words you can find in the newspaper. Ask a friend about these words. Make a note for each word.

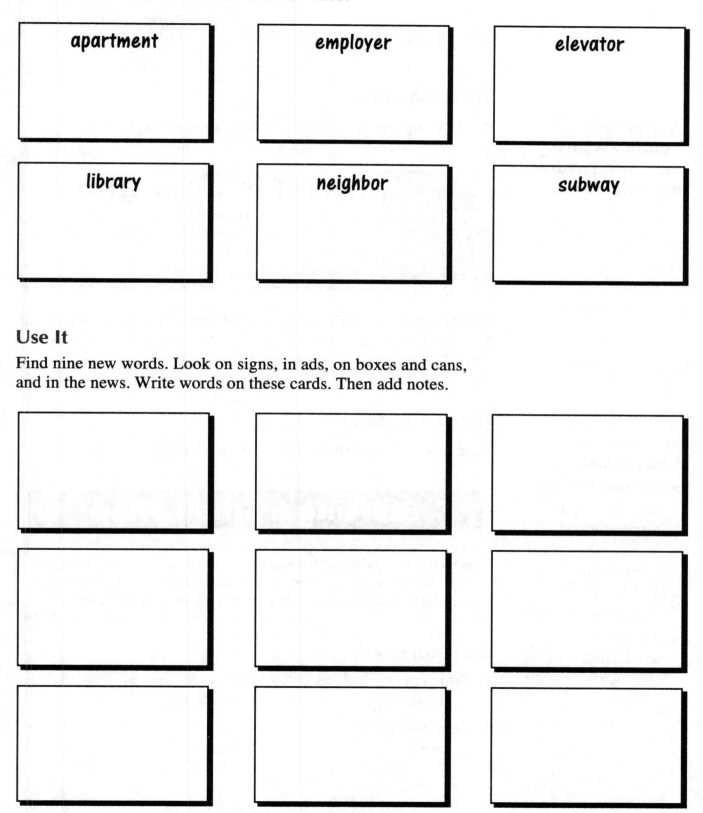

| apartment | employer | elevator |
| library | neighbor | subway |

Use It

Find nine new words. Look on signs, in ads, on boxes and cans, and in the news. Write words on these cards. Then add notes.

Using Clues to Meaning

◆ *Using Context Clues*

A writer may explain a word in the text. A picture may help, too.

This Is the Idea

Read this tip from a cookbook. Think about what gravy is.

Secret of Good Gravy

I love to serve a roast with gravy, which is a sauce made from meat juices and flour. The secret to smooth gravy is a strong arm! You have to stir the lumps out.

Suppose that you don't know the word *gravy*. You see it in the title. But you don't give up because you don't know *gravy*. You look for clues. You find that the writer explains *gravy*. It is a sauce.

Take a Closer Look

Clues to look for

- A wren **is** a bird.
- A wren **is like** a sparrow.
- a wren, **which is** a small bird
- a wren, **or** small bird
- a wren, a small bird,

Read this business article. Think about what capital is.

Starting a Small Shop

So you want to open a shop of your own! Before you do, ask yourself some questions. Do you have the capital, the money, you will need? Are you willing to work long hours? Can you get help? Do you get along well with people? Do you have a good idea for a shop?

Circle your answers.

1. Which phrase follows *capital* and has commas around it?
   a. the money
   b. long hours

2. What is capital?
   a. money
   b. time

Try It

Read this safety warning. Think about what a hazard is.

Caution: Shock Hazard!

We hope you like your new hair dryer. Please be careful when you use it. We have made it as safe as we can, but you should know about a hazard, or danger. There is a danger of shock. Take great care not to use the dryer near water. Do not use it when you stand or sit in water.

Circle your answers.

1. What is a hazard?
   a. a danger   b. a warning

2. Which of these is a hazard?
   a. dry hair   b. a shock

Use It

Read this science article. Think about what a pupil and an iris are.

How Light Gets into the Eye

Take a close look at your eye. Notice the black circle at the center. It is the *pupil*, the opening that lets light into the eye. Around it is a colored ring. That is the *iris*, a muscle (MUSS-ul) that opens and closes the pupil. The iris may be blue, brown, gray, or green. It gives your eyes their color.

Circle your answers.

1. What is the text about?
   a. how to choose glasses   b. how light gets into the eye

2. What is the pupil?
   a. an opening   b. a muscle

3. What is the iris?
   a. an opening   b. a muscle

4. What does the iris do?
   a. opens and closes the pupil   b. makes the eye black

Thinking What You'll Read

Predicting Content

Before you start to read, think about what you'll read. That will help you get ready to read.

This Is the Idea

Read the title and the words below the title. Look at the picture. Think about what is likely to be in the text.

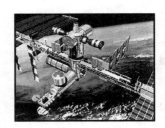

A VISIT TO THE

Space Station

How Does It Feel to Be in Orbit?

When you think about what you'll read, you might picture a rocket or a space suit or the Earth as it looks from space. To get ready to read, you might write these words on a sheet of paper:

rocket   space shuttle   liftoff

Take a Closer Look

Read the title and the words below the title. Look at the picture. Think about what is likely to be in the text.

What to do
- Picture what you will read about.
- List words about your idea.
- Look for words about your idea in the text.

Be Kind to Your Ears!

Loud Sounds Can Cause Hearing Loss

Which words are likely to be in the text? Circle them.

earphones   volume   sunshine   music

Try It

Read the title and the words below the title. Look at the picture.
Think about what is likely to be in the text.

Using Your New Phone

Everything You Need to Know

List words that are likely to be in the text.

_____   _____

_____   _____

_____   _____

Use It

Read the title and the words below the title. Look at the picture.
Think about what is likely to be in the text.

Do You Need a **Loan?** *You Can Borrow for the Things You Need*

Circle your answers.

1. Which is the text more likely to tell you?
   a. how to choose a car that's right for you
   b. how much you can borrow to buy a car

2. Which is the text more likely to tell you?
   a. which month has the coldest weather
   b. how much you'll have to pay each month

3. Which is the text more likely to tell you?
   a. how to ask for a loan
   b. how to ask for a job at the bank

Thinking Why You'll Read

◆ *Setting a Purpose*

Think about why you will read. Do you want to learn something? What do you want to learn? As you read, keep your reason for reading in mind.

This Is the Idea

Look at this article. Think about why you would read it.

How to Get the Job You Want

Often you read to learn how to do something. Why would you read this article? You would read it to learn how to get a better job. With that in mind, you would watch for good ideas. You might copy some of the best ones.

Take a Closer Look

Read this part of a business article. Think about why you would read the rest of it.

Working and Playing on the Great Lakes

The Great Lakes are important to the United States and Canada. Ships carry goods across the lakes. Visitors tour the lakes for fun. The money from shipping creates jobs. So does the money visitors spend. Let's take a closer look at shipping and touring.

Why would you read the rest? Check two reasons.

_____ a. to learn about the ships that carry goods on the lakes

_____ b. to learn how the lakes were formed and how deep they are

_____ c. to learn about visitors touring the lakes

Try It

Read this part of a column. Think about why you would read the rest.

Let's Keep Music in the Schools

The school budget will have to be cut. What will the school board decide to cut? It must not be the music program, because we need music. Let me tell you why we need music, and let me suggest some other programs that could be cut.

Why would you read the rest? Check two reasons. You would read it to find out the writer's ideas about

_____ a. where to learn to play music

_____ b. why we need music

_____ c. what other programs could be cut

Use It

Read this review of a book. Think about why you would read the book.

Future Hope for a *Cancer Cure*

Reviewed by Brent Wood

Most people know someone who has had cancer. Will this disease ever be cured? This book offers hope. It clearly explains what cancer is and tells how science has tried to find a cure. It tells what has not worked and why it has not worked. It also tells what may work in the future.

Why would you read *Future Hope for a Cancer Cure*? Check five reasons. You would read it to find out

_____ a. who has had cancer

_____ b. what cancer is

_____ c. how science has tried to find a cure

_____ d. what cures have not worked

_____ e. why some cures have not worked

_____ f. what cures may work in the future

Asking the Right Questions

◆ *Questioning the Text*

This Is the Idea

Asking questions helps you get the facts. Asking questions helps you find the most important part of the text.

As you read this part of a science article, ask "What?"

The Eardrum

The eardrum is a part of the ear that's like a tiny drum. It moves quickly when sound waves reach it. Lay a sheet of paper on your hand and bring it close to your mouth. Say "Ahhhh" in a deep voice. Did you feel the paper move? That's how the eardrum moves.

What is the eardrum? It is a part of the ear that's like a tiny drum.

What does the eardrum do? It moves quickly when sound waves reach it.

Take a Closer Look

Ask
- Who?
- What?
- When?
- Where?
- How?
- Why?

As you read this column, ask "Why?"

Safety First, for a Child's Sake

The other day, I saw a child of 4 or 5 standing on the front seat of a moving car. Readers, please tell everyone you know to use a safety seat. For one thing, it's the law for children under 4. More important, though, is the fact that safety seats save lives. Don't put a child at risk!

Why should someone use a safety seat? Check each reason. **Hint:** Find *use a safety seat* in the text. What two reasons come next?

____ a. It's the law.

____ b. Kids like sitting.

____ c. The seats save lives.

____ d. The seats are soft.

Try It

Read this news report. Ask "Who? What? When? Where?"

New Head for City Transit

CENTER CITY —The mayor gave John Chen the job of running Center City Transit today. Mr. Chen wants to make the transit system the most modern in the country. "It won't be easy," he said. "It will take time, but we can do it." New buses will arrive next month, the mayor said.

Circle your answers.

1. Who will be running Center City Transit?
   a. John Chen
   b. the mayor

2. When will new buses arrive?
   a. today
   b. next month

Use It

Read this language article. Ask questions about it.

The Story of a "BIG" Word

Keep an eye out for the word *jumbo*. You may see it at a snack bar. It may describe a thick shake. It may describe a plate of nachos. The word has come to mean "big" because it was the name of an elephant. Jumbo was a star in P. T. Barnum's circus. He was very famous.

Circle your answers.

1. What is *jumbo?*
   a. a word
   b. a snack bar

2. What is a jumbo hamburger?
   a. a thin one
   b. a big one

3. Why did *jumbo* get its meaning?
   a. It was a name.
   b. It was a short word.

4. Who was P. T. Barnum?
   a. someone who cooked
   b. someone who had a circus

Checking as You Read

◆ *Monitoring Comprehension*

**Think about what you already know. Then think about what you want to find out.
As you read, keep track of what you learn.**

This Is the Idea

Read this title of a travel article. What country will it be about?

LET'S LOOK AT BRAZIL

What country will it be about? Brazil.

What do you know about Brazil? What do you want to know?

Take a Closer Look

Jade made this chart about Brazil. Read what is on it.

What I Know	What I Want to Know	What I Learned
A country in South America.	Is it large or small?	
Warm climate.	What is the capital?	
Many people there speak Portuguese.	What countries are near it?	

1. What does Jade already know about Brazil? Circle your answer.
   Hint: Look at the left part of the chart.
   a. where it is   b. how big it is

2. What does Jade want to know about Brazil? Circle your answer.
   Hint: Look at the middle part of the chart.
   a. what its capital is   b. what products Brazil sells

Try It

Look at this chart about Brazil. Think about what should go on it.

What I Know	What I Want to Know	What I Learned

1. Let's say that you know this about Brazil. Put it on the chart.
   It is the largest country in South America.

2. You want to know this about Brazil. Put it on the chart.
   Is it one of the largest countries in the world?

3. What else do you know about Brazil? Put it on the chart.

4. What do you want to know? Put it on the chart.

Use It

Now read about Brazil. What new things do you learn?

Brazil is a country in South America.

Brazil is the fifth-largest country in the world. It is so large that it fills almost half of South America. There are 12 other countries in South America. Ten share borders with Brazil. Most of the people in Brazil live near the coast. The capital is not near the coast, though. It is inland. It is called Brasilia.

Coffee is a major product in Brazil. More coffee comes from Brazil than from any other country in the world.

Add the things you learned to the chart above.

Putting It in a Few Words

◆ *Summarizing*

As you read, pause now and then. Think about what you've read. Sum it up. Put it in a few words.

This Is the Idea

Read this fitness tip. Think about how to put it in a few words.

> # WALKING FOR FITNESS
> Walking is the best way to keep fit. It helps keep your weight down, and it tones your muscles. Even your arms get a workout if you move them as you walk. Walking keeps the bones in your legs and hips strong. It isn't jarring, as running can be.

How could you sum that up? You could put it in these few words: "Walking keeps weight down, tones muscles, keeps bones strong, and isn't jarring."

Take a Closer Look

To sum it up
- Keep what's most important.
- Cut all the rest.

Read this home safety tip. Think about how to sum it up.

> ## A "Timely" Tip
> Here's a good idea. Twice a year we reset our clocks. In the spring, we turn them ahead to start daylight savings time. In the fall, we turn them back to standard time. Each time you reset your clocks, change the batteries in your smoke alarms. If you do, they'll always be fresh.

Which sentence does the best job of putting the tip in a few words? Circle your answer. *Hint:* Choose the one that has what's important and *only* what's important.

a. We reset our clocks twice a year.

b. Change alarm batteries when you reset your clocks.

c. Don't forget to reset your clocks in spring and fall.

Try It

Read this part of a handbook for voters. Sum it up in your mind.

> **Q.** How long do people in Center City hold office?
>
> **A.** The mayor serves for four years. (This wasn't always the case. In the city's early years, mayors served six years per term.)
> Members of the City Council serve for two years. (Years ago, the mayor could choose council members. Now the voters choose them.)

The question is "How long do people hold office?" Check two sentences that you would use to sum up the answer.

_____ a. The mayor serves for four years.

_____ b. The mayor used to choose council members.

_____ c. City Council members serve for two years.

Use It

Read this part of a life story. Think about how to sum it up.

> # THE TWO CAREERS OF CLARE BOOTHE LUCE
>
> Clare Boothe Luce was born in New York City. She was a writer and public servant. She wrote articles. She wrote plays, too. All of her plays became movies. She served in Congress for four years. She lived a long life. She died at the age of 84.

Here are four ways that readers might sum up "The Two Careers of Clare Boothe Luce." Circle the best one.

a. Clare Boothe Luce was born in New York City. She lived a long life. She died at the age of 84.

b. Clare Boothe Luce was a writer and public servant. She wrote articles and plays that became movies. She served in Congress.

c. Clare Boothe Luce lived a long life. She served in Congress for four years. She died at 84.

d. Clare Boothe Luce was a writer. She wrote articles and plays. All of her plays became movies.

Finding What It's About

Most news reports are about one topic. Most charts, ads, and articles are about one topic.

This Is the Idea

Read these headlines. What are they about?

The headline on the left is about hot weather. Notice that it shows a person who is hot and uses the word *heat*. The topic is hot weather.

The headline on the right is about cold weather. It shows a person who is cold and uses the word *cold*. The topic is cold weather.

Take a Closer Look

Read this part of a chart. What is it about?

What shows the topic?

- a title
- headings
- a headline
- words used again and again

Long Rivers of the World

RIVERS	HOW LONG
Nile	4,145 miles
Amazon	4,000 miles
Yangtze	3,915 miles

Circle your answers.

1. Which words are in both the title and headings? *Hint:* They are in blue ink.
   a. *world* and *how*   b. *long* and *rivers*

2. What is the topic?
   a. long rivers   b. the Amazon River

Try It

Read this part of a travel article. What is it about?

Mount Rushmore

Visit Mount Rushmore

Mount Rushmore is in South Dakota. It is made of a hard rock called granite. The heads of four presidents are carved in the rock. They are Washington, Jefferson, Lincoln, and Teddy Roosevelt. Each head is about 50 feet high. They were carved by Gutzon Borglum and his helpers.

Circle your answers.

1. Which of these is in the title?
   a. Gutzon Borglum
   b. Mount Rushmore

2. Which of these is below the picture?
   a. South Dakota
   b. Mount Rushmore

3. Which of these is the topic?
   a. Mount Rushmore
   b. granite rock

Use It

Read this part of a life story. What is it about?

Sidney Bechet, A Giant of Jazz

Sidney Bechet

Sidney Bechet was a great jazz musician. He was born in New Orleans. He played in the band led by "King" Oliver. Later, he played in Duke Ellington's band. He led a band of his own, too. He lived the last part of his life in France.

Circle your answers.

1. Which of these is in the title?
   a. Sidney Bechet
   b. "King" Oliver

2. Which of these is below the picture?
   a. Duke Ellington
   b. Sidney Bechet

3. Which of these is the topic?
   a. great jazz musicians
   b. Sidney Bechet

Using the Topic

◆ *Anchoring Understanding on the Topic*

First, think about what the topic is. (See Lesson 9.) Keep the topic in mind as you read. Focus on what is important to the topic.

This Is the Idea

Lena made this list. Which items are about the topic?

My Office Skills

planning	filing
typing	soccer
jogging	using a computer

Lena wanted the list to be about her office skills. That was the topic she had in mind. Most of the things on the list are about the topic "office skills." The ones in black ink are not.

Take a Closer Look

As you read, ask yourself

• Is this about the topic?
• Is this important to the topic?

Read these directions. Which parts are most important to the topic?

HOW TO PLACE YOUR ORDER

Your order is important to us. We want to get your order to you as quickly as we can. Be sure to put your address on the order form. Send the form in the brown envelope. Be sure to include a check. Thanks for your order! Have a nice day!

Check two statements that are important to the topic.
Hint: The topic is "how to place an order."

_____ a. Your order is important to us.

_____ b. Be sure to put your address on the order form.

_____ c. Be sure to include a check.

_____ d. Thanks for your order!

Try It

Read this profile. Which parts are about the topic?

Library of Congress,
Prints & Photographs Division,
Carl Van Vechten collection
[LC-USZ62-117880]

Bessie Smith

Bessie Smith, Queen of the Blues

Bessie Smith was a great blues singer. Ma Rainey was also a great blues singer. Smith had a very strong voice. She sang with great power and feeling. Smith recorded songs with Louis Armstrong. Armstrong played the trumpet. Smith also wrote many blues songs.

The topic is Bessie Smith. Check two statements that are about her.

_____ a. Ma Rainey was also a great blues singer.

_____ b. Smith had a very strong voice.

_____ c. Smith recorded songs with Louis Armstrong.

_____ d. Armstrong played the trumpet.

Use It

Read this business advice. Which parts are about the topic?

Express Shoes

Loafers $19.99
Pumps $25.00
Total $54.99
PAID

Keep That Receipt

Shoes are on sale. They're a good bargain. You buy a pair. You get a receipt. It's a little piece of paper, but it's important. It proves that you paid for what you bought. Keep that receipt. You may need it. You will need that receipt if you want to return the shoes for some reason.

Circle your answers.

1. What is the advice about?
   a. shoes   b. receipts

2. Which of these is about the topic?
   a. Shoes are on sale.   b. Keep that receipt.

3. Which sentence is more important to the topic?
   a. They're a good bargain.   b. You may need it.

Finding the Writer's Point

This Is the Idea

Writers sometimes state a point in a sentence.

Read this health advice. Look for the writer's point.

You and Tooth Care

Tooth care begins with you. Daily brushing is a must. You should brush after every meal, but at the very least brush twice a day. In addition, you should floss daily. Flossing removes bits of food between the teeth where your brush can't reach.

The advice is about what you can do to take care of your teeth. That is the topic. The title states it. The text in black ink is about ways to care for your teeth at home. The sentence in blue ink is about all the other sentences. It states the writer's point.

Take a Closer Look

Look for a statement of the point
- in the first sentence
- in the last sentence

Read this health advice. Look for the writer's point.

Your Dentist and Tooth Care

An exam in a dentist's office helps stop trouble before it starts. During an exam, the dentist can spot problems while they are small and easy to fix. The exam can help prevent big problems. You should see your dentist twice a year for an exam.

Circle your answer.

1. What is the advice about? *Hint:* Read the title.
   a. spotting small problems   b. dentists and tooth care

Underline your answer in the text.

2. Which sentence states the writer's point?
   Hints: Read the first sentence. Read the last sentence.

Try It

Read this how-to article. Look for the writer's point.

Measure with Care

Suppose that you want to get a new sofa. You find one you like, and you buy it. When it arrives at your home, it won't fit through the door! You didn't measure to see if it would fit. If you measure, you will save time, effort, and money.

Circle your answers.

1. What is the article about?
   a. why you should measure with care
   b. how to choose a sofa for your home

2. Which sentence states the writer's point?
   a. If you measure, you will save time, effort, and money.
   b. Suppose that you want to get a new sofa.

Use It

Read this movie review. Look for the writer's point.

Ana Is a Delight

This movie will warm the heart of any viewer. It tells the story of a young woman in Cleveland. Ana thinks life is a joy, and she tries to make the people she knows feel the way she does. She does kind things for people. She also plays little tricks on them to make them smile.

Circle your answers.

1. What is the review about?
   a. a movie that will make people feel afraid
   b. a movie that will warm people's hearts

2. Which sentence states the writer's point?
   a. This movie will warm the heart of any viewer.
   b. It tells the story of a young woman in Cleveland.
   c. She does kind things for people.
   d. She also plays little tricks on them to make them smile.

Using the Writer's Point

◆ *Anchoring Understanding on the Main Idea*

This Is the Idea

Read this election ad. Which parts are about the writer's point?

★ Vote for Gaspar Guzmán ★

Gaspar Guzmán deserves your vote. Guzmán is honest. He knows how to get the job done. Guzmán held an exciting rally last week. Voting is your right and your civic duty. Don't forget to go to the polls on Tuesday.

The ad asks you to vote for Gaspar Guzmán. The first sentence states the writer's point. The next two sentences are about the writer's point. The ones in blue ink are not.

Take a Closer Look

Read these hints. Which parts help make the writer's point?

WHAT TO DO WHEN THERE'S TOO MUCH TO DO

There never seems to be enough time, does there? Make a plan to make the best use of your time. First list all the things you have to do. Then number them in the order that they're due. (Don't you hate deadlines?) Start working on number one, and go on from there.

Check two statements that help make the writer's point. *Hint:* The writer's point is "Make a plan to make the best use of your time."

_____ a. There never seems to be enough time, does there?

_____ b. First list all the things you have to do.

_____ c. Then number them in the order that they're due.

_____ d. (Don't you hate deadlines?)

Try It

Read this column. What is the writer's point?

Advertise Your Sale

You cleaned the attic. You cleaned the garage. Now you're going to have a tag sale, yard sale, or garage sale. Make sure that people know about your sale. Post signs in the neighborhood. Leave flyers in local shops. Call friends and neighbors. That's how to make your sale a success.

The writer's point is "Make sure that people know about your sale."
Check two statements that are about that point.

_____ a. You cleaned the attic.

_____ b. You cleaned the garage.

_____ c. Post signs in the neighborhood.

_____ d. Leave flyers in local shops.

Use It

Read this cooking tip. What is the writer's point?

Cooking Fish the Right Way

You've gone fishing and you've been lucky. Fresh fish is so good! Be sure to cook those fish right. If you cook them too long, they will be dry. If your pan isn't hot enough, they'll be mushy. Cook them right. Cook fish quickly in a hot pan.

Check your answers.

1. What is the point of the tip?

   _____ a. You've gone fishing, and you've been lucky.

   _____ b. Cook fish quickly in a hot pan.

2. Which two sentences are more important to the point?

   _____ a. You've gone fishing, and you've been lucky.

   _____ b. If you cook them too long, they will be dry.

   _____ c. If your pan isn't hot enough, they'll be mushy.

Finding Useful Details

◆ *Recognizing Significant Details*

Details are the little things in a piece of writing. Some details are more useful than others.

This Is the Idea

Read this notice. Which details are most useful?

MISSING CAT

Tess is gray. She is a very big cat. Her tail is thick and fluffy. I have two other cats. She is wearing a collar. My phone number is on her tag.

Most of the details are useful. They would help you decide if you had seen the missing cat. The sentence in black ink is not useful. That detail would not help you spot the missing cat.

Take a Closer Look

Look for useful details about the health value of Toasty Oats.

As you read, ask yourself
• Is this detail useful?
• Is this a detail that I need to know?

Toasty Oats, the Healthy Treat

You'll love Toasty Oats in your breakfast bowl! They are all natural. We make them from whole oats. No salt is added. We sweeten them with fruit juice. You made a great choice. Toasty Oats are yummy!

Which sentences state a useful detail about the health value of Toasty Oats? Check each one.

_____ a. You'll love Toasty Oats in your breakfast bowl!

_____ b. We make them from whole oats.

_____ c. We sweeten them with fruit juice.

_____ d. Toasty Oats are yummy!

Try It

Read these directions. Which details are most useful?

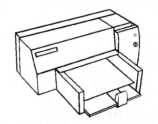

$25 REBATE OFFER

Thank you for buying the new Swifty 50 Printer. To show our thanks, we'll send you a $25 rebate check. Send us the bar code from the box. Send a copy of the store receipt, too. Be sure to include your name and address.

Which details do you need to know to get the refund?
Check each one.

____ a. Thank you for buying the new Swifty 50 Printer.

____ b. Send us the bar code from the box.

____ c. Send a copy of the store receipt, too.

____ d. Be sure to include your name and address.

Use It

Find the details that would be most useful in entering the contest.

Win a Trip to Paris!

You can win a week in Paris! You'll fly there and back on the Concorde. You'll stay in a first-class hotel. To enter, just tell us why you want to go to Paris. Write your reasons on a postcard. Send it to the address on the back of this sheet. You must send it before June 10. Good luck!

Which details do you need to know to enter the contest?
Check each one.

____ a. You can win a week in Paris!

____ b. You'll fly there and back on the Concorde.

____ c. You'll stay in a first-class hotel.

____ d. To enter, just tell us why you want to go to Paris.

____ e. Write your reasons on a postcard.

____ f. Send it to the address on the back of this sheet.

____ g. You must send it before June 10.

____ h. Good luck!

Using Details

Some details are more useful than others. Some details help you do something.

This Is the Idea

Read this advice. Which details will help you buy running shoes?

Shopping for Running Shoes

When you buy running shoes, choose shoes that fit your feet. Running shoes come in countless styles. They come in a rainbow of colors. There are dozens of brands. Choose shoes that are not tight and not loose. Walk in them to see if they support your foot.

The advice is about choosing running shoes. The writer says that you should choose shoes that fit. The details in blue ink will help you do that. The details in black ink will not help.

Take a Closer Look

Read these hints. Which details will help you save money?

As you read, ask yourself
- Is this detail useful in doing something?
- What makes this detail useful?

—— Start the Savings Habit ——

It's hard to save. Here's a simple plan to get you started. Every night, put your pocket change in a jar. When the jar is full, open a savings account. Start filling the jar again. Each time it's full, put the money into your account. This worked for me, and it can work for you.

Check two details that will help you save money. *Hint:* They are the ones that tell you just what to do.

_____ a. Every night, put your pocket change in a jar.

_____ b. It's hard to save.

_____ c. This worked for me, and it can work for you.

_____ d. When the jar is full, open a savings account.

Try It

Read this how-to column. Which details help you do something?

How to Fix a Leaking Faucet

You hear it all night long: drip, drip, drip. You've got to fix that leaking faucet. Most of the time, a leaking faucet needs a new washer. You can get a washer at a hardware store. Notice the brand name on your faucet. Notice the model number. Get a washer for that brand and model.

What will this column help you do? Fix a leaking faucet.
Check three details that will help you do that.

_____ a. Notice the brand name on your faucet.

_____ b. You hear it all night long: drip, drip, drip.

_____ c. Notice the model number.

_____ d. Get a washer for that brand and model.

Use It

Read this health advice. Which details help you do something?

GOOD NIGHT, SLEEP TIGHT

Are you having trouble sleeping? Most people have trouble sleeping now and then. These hints may help. Don't drink coffee before bedtime. Darken the room where you sleep. Make the room quieter. Get rid of your worries before you go to bed. Good night. Sweet dreams.

1. What will "Good Night, Sleep Tight" help you do?
   Check your answer.

   _____ a. get rid of your worries

   _____ b. sleep better

2. Which two details will help you do that? Check them.

   _____ a. Darken the room where you sleep.

   _____ b. Don't drink coffee before bed.

   _____ c. Most people have trouble sleeping now and then.

Finding When It Happens

♦ *Following a Sequence*

This Is the Idea

Read this recipe. As you read, notice *First, Next,* and *Then.*

Three-Step Corn Muffins

First, mix.   Next, pour.   Then, bake.

You should mix the batter first. Why? That step is on the left and begins with the word *First*. You should bake the muffins last. Why? That step is on the right and makes sense as the final step.

Take a Closer Look

What shows order?
- left to right
- top to bottom
- key words like *after, finally, first, last, next, then,* and *when*

As you read this news report, notice *First, Next,* and *Finally.*

Debate Format Is Set

NEW CITY — Three people are running for mayor. They have agreed to a debate and have agreed on a format. First, each person will speak alone. Next, they will all answer questions from the press. Finally, they will make closing statements.

What will happen first in the debate? Circle your answer.
Hint: Which is first in the report and begins with *First?*
    a. each speaking alone   b. questions from the press

Try It

Read these directions. Notice the order of the steps.

Here's How to Fix a Broken Plate

First, be sure that the pieces are clean. Next, put a little glue on each piece. Let the glue dry until it is sticky. Then press the pieces together for a minute. After the glue has dried for an hour, you can use the plate.

Number these steps to show the right order.

_____ Let the glue dry until it is sticky.

_____ Put a little glue on each piece.

_____ Wait an hour.

_____ Press the pieces together for a minute.

_____ Be sure that the pieces are clean.

Use It

Read this news report. Notice the order of the events.

Spill Snarls Traffic

NEW CITY — Olive oil stopped traffic today when a truck full of oil began to leak. Oil ran onto the street. Drivers couldn't stop their cars. First one car slid into the truck. Then a second car slid into the first. Soon more cars slid into one another. They were all going slowly, so no one was hurt. When tow trucks arrived, they could not take the cars away. The tow trucks slid, too. Finally, firefighters washed the oil away. After that, traffic could move again.

Number these steps to show the right order.

_____ Firefighters washed the oil away.

_____ Tow trucks slid in the oil.

_____ Olive oil ran onto the street.

_____ Traffic could move again.

_____ Cars slid into one another.

Using Time Order

Notice the order of steps or events. Think about why they happen in that order.

This Is the Idea

Read this cooking tip. Why are the steps in this order?

Onions Without Tears

Do onions make you cry? Here's how to peel and slice an onion without tears. First, fill a pot or bowl with cold water. Then peel the onion in the water. Remove the peel so that it doesn't get in your way. Now slice the onion in the water. You'll have a sliced onion and no tears.

The tip tells you to peel an onion in a pot of water. Would the tip work if you peeled the onion before you filled the pot with water? Of course not. The tip won't work if the steps are out of order.

Take a Closer Look

Read this news report. Why did the events happen in this order?

As you read, ask yourself

- Why are the steps in this order?
- Why did the events happen in this order?

Child Saved from Fire

CENTER CITY — Fire broke out on 7th Street before dawn. When a neighbor saw the fire, she called 911. Firefighters arrived within minutes. At first, people told them that no one was in the building. Then they saw a girl in a window. They rushed in and brought her out.

Circle your answers. *Hint:* Think about which answer makes sense.

1. Why didn't the firefighters arrive before the neighbor called?
   a. They were busy.
   b. They didn't know about the fire.

2. Why didn't the firefighters rush into the building right away?
   a. They thought that no one was in the building.
   b. They saw a girl in a window.

Try It

Read these directions. Why are the steps in this order?

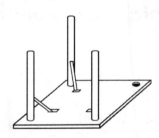

Assemble Your Table in Four Steps

1 Check to see that all the parts are in the package.

2 Insert the legs into the holes in the top.

3 Use screws to attach a brace to each leg.

4 Use screws to attach each brace to the top.

Circle your answers.

1. What might go wrong if you skip step 1?
   a. Later you might find that some part is missing.
   b. You will have a hard time getting the legs into the holes.

2. What might go wrong if you do step 2 last?
   a. You will have a hard time getting the legs into the holes.
   b. You won't have enough screws.

Use It

Read this news report. Why did the events happen in this order?

Bridge Failure in Center City

CENTER CITY — Early in the morning, some boats were headed up North River. The bridge keeper raised the drawbridge. The boats went through. The bridge would not go down. Traffic backed up for two miles. At last the bridge was repaired and traffic could move again.

Circle your answers.

1. The bridge keeper tried to lower the bridge. When did that probably happen?
   a. Before the boats went through.
   b. After the boats went through.

2. Drivers stopped their cars at the bridge. When did that probably happen?
   a. Before the bridge keeper raised the drawbridge.
   b. After the bridge keeper raised the drawbridge.

Finding Why It Happens

◆ *Recognizing Cause and Effect*

To find a cause, ask "Why?"

This Is the Idea

Read this warning label. As you read, ask "Why?"

> ## Side Effects You Should Know About
>
> Always take these pills with a full glass of water. If you do not, then you may feel stomach pain. Do not take more than one pill. If you do, then you may feel dizzy. If you feel dizzy, then lie down until the feeling is gone.

Why may you feel stomach pain? If you do not take these pills with a full glass of water.

Why may you feel dizzy? If you take more than one pill.

Take a Closer Look

These words help you find causes

- *because:* This happened because that happened.
- *if . . . then:* If this happens, then that will happen.

Read this part of a science article. As you read, ask "Why?"

> **Q** What causes hiccups?
>
> **A** You hiccup because a muscle inside you twitches. The muscle is between your chest and your stomach. The muscle helps you breathe by pulling when you breathe in and pushing when you breathe out. If you eat too quickly, then the muscle twitches—and you hiccup.

Circle your answers.

1. Why do you hiccup?
   a. You breathe.   b. A muscle twitches.

2. Why does the muscle twitch?
   a. You breathe.   b. You eat too quickly.

Try It

Read this opinion column. As you read, ask "Why?"

Pay Farmers to Harvest the Wind

Let's pay farmers to "plant" windmills. If a farmer put up a windmill, then the farmer would get a payment. We would use less oil because we would use more wind power. We would help farmers keep their farms, too.

Circle your answers.

1. Why would a farmer get a payment?
   a. for putting up a windmill   b. for keeping a farm

2. Why would we use less oil?
   a. We'd use more wind power.   b. Prices would be low.

Use It

Read this business article. As you read, ask "Why?"

SUPPLY AND DEMAND

The new Wolf sports car is just out. Everyone wants one because they look so cute. There aren't enough to go around because Wolf Motors made only a few. The demand for Wolf cars is high. The supply of Wolf cars is low. Wolf dealers will charge a high price, and many people will pay it. That's the law of supply and demand. If demand is high and supply is low, then prices go up.

Circle your answers.

1. Why does everyone want a Wolf sports car?
   a. The price is high.   b. They're cute.

2. Why aren't there enough to go around?
   a. Wolf Motors made only a few.   b. The price is high.

3. What will happen because supply is low and demand is high?
   a. Prices will go down.   b. Prices will go up.

Using Reasons

◆ **Understanding Cause and Effect**

As you read, think about why things happen. Look for a cause. A cause makes something happen.

This Is the Idea

As you read this history article, look for causes.

The Dust Bowl of Kansas

Long ago on the fields of Kansas, grasses held the soil in place. Then farmers plowed the fields to plant crops, and the grasses were gone. For a long time, no rain fell, so the soil dried out. Then great winds blew the soil away, and dust filled the air.

Why did farmers plow the fields? To plant crops.

What made the soil dry out? The fact that no rain fell.

What caused dust to fill the air? The great winds that blew.

Take a Closer Look

As you read this health report, look for causes.

To think about causes, ask yourself

- Why did that happen?
- What made that happen?
- What caused that?

Some Foods Cause Trouble

We all need to eat, of course, but some foods cause trouble for some people. For example, some people can't eat peanuts. If they do, they may begin to wheeze. They may have so much trouble breathing that they have to be rushed to a hospital.

Circle your answers.

1. What causes some people to begin to wheeze?
   Hint: What comes just before "If they do"?
   a. eating peanuts
   b. breathing

2. What would cause them to be rushed to a hospital?
   a. trouble breathing
   b. trouble swallowing

Try It

As you read this science article, look for causes.

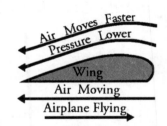

How Wings Work ———————————————

Hold a small piece of paper in front of your mouth. Blow over the paper. The paper will rise up. Why? The moving air above the paper makes the pressure lower. The pressure below the paper is greater. The greater pressure pushes the paper up. That's how an airplane's wing works.

Circle your answers.

1. What causes the paper to rise?
   a. Still air above it makes the pressure lower.
   b. Moving air above it makes the pressure lower.

2. What will happen if you stop blowing?
   a. The paper will keep rising.
   b. The paper will fall or droop.

Use It

Read this nature article. Look for causes.

Why Honeybees *Dance*

When a bee finds food, it gathers some and flies back to the hive. At the hive, the bee dances for the other bees. The bee's dance tells the others where the food is. One part of the dance shows which way to fly. Another part shows how far to fly.

Circle your answers.

1. Why would one bee dance for other bees?
   a. to make them feel happy
   b. to tell them where food is
   c. to get into the hive

2. Why would the other bees fly toward the east?
   a. because they were confused
   b. because they always fly toward the east
   c. because the dance told them to go that way

Finding Groups

◆ *Recognizing Classification*

Most things in groups are alike in some way. Notice how they are alike. Think about other things that might fit in the group.

This Is the Idea

Read these lists. Notice how the things in each group are alike.

This Week's Center City Job Listing

Full-Time
▶ head cook, daily
▶ fry cook, 5 days
▶ manager, 6 days

Part-Time
▶ cleanup crew, 2 hours, nights
▶ waiters, 4-hour shifts
▶ host, 2 days a week

The jobs are listed in two groups. If you wanted a job for a few hours each evening, you would look in the part-time list.

Take a Closer Look

Read this chart of bus fares. Think about who belongs in each group.

CENTER CITY BUS FARES	
General	$1.25
Seniors over 65 (with valid ID)	$.75
Students (with valid ID)	$.50
Children under 5	free

Circle your answers. *Hint:* In each case, first think about what group the person fits in. Then check the chart to find the fare.

1. How much would a baby have to pay?
   a. $1.25   b. 75 cents   c. 50 cents   d. nothing

2. How much would a man of 70 have to pay? He has a driver's license that shows his date of birth.
   a. $1.25   b. 75 cents   c. 50 cents   d. nothing

Try It

As you read this rate chart, notice how cars are grouped.

| Daily Car Rental Rates | Compact $50 | Full-Size $65 | Van $70 |

Compact includes: Nimble 2000, Saver GX, Raven GT
Full-Size includes: Granite 9000, Boulder XL, Rhino GT

Circle your answers.

1. What will it cost to rent a Nimble 2000 for a day?
   a. $50　　　　b. $65　　　　c. $70

2. What will it cost to rent a Boulder XL for a day?
   a. $50　　　　b. $65　　　　c. $70

Use It

As you read this rate chart, notice how cars are grouped.

Car Rental Rates

	COMPACT	FULL-SIZE	VAN
Day	$ 50	$ 65	$ 70
Weekend	75	95	105
Week	300	390	420

COMPACT INCLUDES: Nimble 2000, Saver GX, Raven GT
FULL-SIZE INCLUDES: Granite 9000, Boulder XL, Rhino GT

Circle your answers.

1. What will it cost to rent a Raven GT for a week?
   a. $75　　　　b. $300　　　　c. $70

2. What will it cost to rent a Granite 9000 for a weekend?
   a. $50　　　　b. $95　　　　c. $420

3. What will it cost to rent a van for a day?
   a. $50　　　　b. $65　　　　c. $70

Using Groups

♦ *Understanding Classification*

**As you read,
notice groups.
Writers usually
have reasons for
making groups.
Think about the
writer's reasons.
Think about what
the groups mean
to you.**

This Is the Idea

Read this bank sign. Think about why it puts forms of ID in groups.

TO CASH A CHECK
You must have two forms of ID.

We will accept
▶ a driver's license
▶ a major credit card
▶ a student ID card with photo

We will not accept
▶ club cards
▶ a Social Security card
▶ a library card

The sign puts forms of ID into two groups. Why? To show what ID the bank will take. What do these groups mean to you? If you want to cash a check, you must have ID from the group in blue ink.

Take a Closer Look

Read this part of a loan form. Why are reasons for loans in groups?

**As you read,
ask yourself**

• Why did the
  writer put things
  in groups?

• What do the
  groups mean
  to me?

Why do you want a loan? Check one.

_____ to buy something (such as a car or house)

_____ to pay debts (such as credit card or school loan)

_____ for home repairs (such as painting or plastering)

Circle your answers. *Hint:* Think about what group your reason belongs in.

1. If you want to fix leaks in your house, what should you check?
   a. to buy something   b. for home repairs

2. If you want to get a new stove, what should you check?
   a. to pay debts   b. to buy something

Try It

Read this cooking article. Think about why it puts foods in groups.

Two Food Bargains

Two of the biggest food bargains are nuts and beans. Nuts include almonds, walnuts, and cashews. There are black, red, pinto, and garbanzo beans. Nuts are a good source of protein. So are beans. Nuts are high in fat, but their fat is good for the heart. Beans are very low in fat.

Circle your answers.

1. If you want a good source of protein, you could choose
   a. almonds   b. red beans   c. either

2. If you want a food that is low in fat, you could choose
   a. walnuts   b. pinto beans   c. either

Use It

Read this rate chart. Think about why it puts cable channels in groups.

Center City Cable	Center City Cable TV Company			
	$90 level	**$120 level**	**$170 level**	
	local channels	local channels	local channels	AllWeather
	AllNews	AllNews	AllNews	Cooking
	BestMovies	BestMovies	BestMovies	
		AllSports	AllSports	

Circle your answers.

1. You want to get the AllNews channel. What is the least you can pay?
   a. $90   b. $120   c. $170

2. You want to get the AllNews and Cooking channels. What is the least you can pay?
   a. $90   b. $120   c. $170

3. You want to get the BestMovies and AllSports channels. What is the least you can pay?
   a. $90   b. $120   c. $170

Finding Likenesses

◆ *Recognizing Comparison*

A writer may tell how things are alike.

This Is the Idea

Read this article. How are Earth and Mars alike?

> Earth and Mars are both planets, and both go around the sun, but Earth is closer to the sun. A year on Earth lasts 365 days, but a year on Mars is much longer—687 days. A day on Earth lasts 24 hours, but a day on Mars is a half hour longer. Both Earth and Mars have moons. However, Mars has two moons to Earth's one.

How are Earth and Mars alike? Both are planets, both go around the sun, and both have moons. The word *both* helps you find the ways that they are alike.

Take a Closer Look

What shows that things are alike

- the same words used to describe the things
- the words *both* and *same*

Read this shopping advice. How are the two grills alike?

> ## Gas Grill or Charcoal Grill?
>
> Both gas and charcoal grills come in many sizes and shapes. They cost about the same to run, but gas grills cost more to buy. Gas grills are easier to use and less messy. Charcoal grills are lighter and easier to move around. It's your choice!

Check the two that tell how gas and charcoal grills are alike. *Hint:* Look for the words *both* and *same* in the text.

_____ a. They come in many sizes and shapes.

_____ b. They cost about the same to run.

_____ c. They cost about the same to buy.

Try It

Read this buyers' guide. How are the two cars alike?

TWO GAS SAVERS

We tested the Splash and Breeze side by side. Both get very good gas mileage. Their list prices are almost the same. How can you choose between them? The Splash is better made. The Breeze is better looking. The Splash is larger and heavier, but the Breeze holds more people.

Check the two that tell how the two cars are alike.

_____ a. They are the same size and weight.

_____ b. They get good gas mileage.

_____ c. They have almost the same list price.

Use It

Read this news report. How are the twins alike?

Twins Meet After Years Apart

CENTER CITY — Kei and Kin are twins. When they were infants, they were adopted by different families. Last week they met for the first time. They found that they both play the flute. They drive the same kind of car. They are both teachers, but they teach different subjects. Kei teaches English. Kin teaches science. They both like ice cream. However, Kei's favorite is peach and Kin prefers chocolate.

Check the four items that tell how Kei and Kin are alike.

_____ a. They were adopted by the same family.

_____ b. Each met the other last week.

_____ c. They play the flute.

_____ d. They drive the same kind of car.

_____ e. They are teachers.

_____ f. They teach science.

_____ g. They like chocolate ice cream best.

Finding Differences

◆ *Recognizing Contrast*

A writer may tell how things are different.

This Is the Idea

Read this article. How are Earth and Mars different?

> Earth and Mars are both planets, and both go around the sun, but Earth is closer to the sun. A year on Earth lasts 365 days, but a year on Mars is much longer—687 days. A day on Earth lasts 24 hours, but a day on Mars is a half hour longer. Both Earth and Mars have moons. However, Mars has two moons to Earth's one.

How are Earth and Mars different? Their distance from the sun, their days, their years, and their moons are different. The words *but* and *however* help you see their differences.

Take a Closer Look

Read this shopping advice. How are the two grills different?

Gas Grill or Charcoal Grill?

Both gas and charcoal grills come in many sizes and shapes. They cost about the same to run, but gas grills cost more to buy. Gas grills are easier to use and less messy. Charcoal grills are lighter and easier to move around. It's your choice!

What shows that things are different

- different words used to describe the things
- words that end in er, such as closer, longer, easier, lighter, larger, and heavier
- the words but and however

Which two items tell how the grills are different? Check them. *Hint:* Look for *but* and words that end in *er.*

_____ a. The cost to run them is different.

_____ b. The cost to buy them is different.

_____ c. One is easier to use than the other.

Try It

Read this buyers' guide. How are the two cars different?

TWO GAS SAVERS

We tested the Splash and Breeze side by side. Both get very good gas mileage. Their list prices are almost the same. How can you choose between them? The Splash is better made. The Breeze is better looking. The Splash is larger and heavier, but the Breeze holds more people.

Check the two items that tell how the two cars are different.

_____ a. One is made better than the other.

_____ b. One gets better gas mileage than the other.

_____ c. One holds more people than the other.

Use It

Read this news report. How are the twins different?

Twins Meet After Years Apart

CENTER CITY — Kei and Kin are twins. When they were infants, they were adopted by different families. Last week they met for the first time. They found that they both play the flute. They drive the same kind of car. They are both teachers, but they teach different subjects. Kei teaches English. Kin teaches science. They both like ice cream. However, Kei's favorite is peach and Kin prefers chocolate.

Check the three ways that the report says Kei and Kin are different.

_____ a. They were adopted by different families.

_____ b. They play different instruments.

_____ c. They like different sports.

_____ d. They drive different kinds of car.

_____ e. They teach different subjects.

_____ f. They like different flavors of ice cream.

_____ g. Their eyes are different colors.

Using What You Find

◆ *Understanding Comparison and Contrast*

Look for ways things are alike and ways they are different. (See Lessons 21 and 22.)

This Is the Idea

Read this buying advice. Why is the difference important?

Cash or Charge? *Think Twice*

Think twice the next time a sales clerk asks, "Will that be cash or charge?" Charging may cost more than paying cash. If you pay cash, you're done. You don't owe any more. If you charge, you may also pay fees and interest.

The advice points out one thing that makes paying cash different from charging. Charging may cost more. Is that an important difference? Yes, it is. It's a difference that can save money.

Take a Closer Look

Read this health tip. Why is the likeness important?

Apples or Oranges: Does It Matter?

They don't look alike. They don't taste the same. But they are both great snack choices. Both give you vitamins that your body needs for good health. And both are much better choices than snacks loaded with sugar and fat.

Think about
- what makes things alike
- what makes things different
- why the likenesses and differences are important

Circle your answers. *Hint:* Notice the sentence in blue ink. Think about the main point.

1. How are apples and oranges alike?
   a. They taste the same.   b. They give you vitamins.

2. Why is the likeness important?
   a. for good taste   b. for good health

Try It

Read this travel advice. Why is the difference important?

Two Routes to Upper Falls

Upper Falls Park is a great place to visit at any time of year. You can take Route 9 through rolling hills and quaint little towns. It's slow going but very pretty. Highway 60 will get you there much faster. It's not pretty, and it may be tough on the nerves, but it's the quick way.

Circle your answers.

1. For nice views while you drive, which would you choose?
   a. Route 9   b. Highway 60

2. If you're in a hurry, which would you choose?
   a. Route 9   b. Highway 60

Use It

Read this ad. Why are differences important?

Take the Train to Work

Are you still driving your car to the city? Try the train.

On the train, we'll give you a seat that's wider than the one in your car. It reclines so that you can take a nap. Don't try that in your car. You can read today's paper. You can read a book. Don't try that in your car, either.

When you get to the city in your car, you'll have to park it. When you get to the city on the train, you can forget about it. We'll park it for you.

Circle your answers.

1. If you wanted to get work done on the way to the city, which would you choose?
   a. your car   b. the train

2. If you wanted to get some rest on the way to the city, which would you choose?
   a. your car   b. the train

Thinking What Will Happen

Predicting Outcomes

As you read, think about what may happen as time passes.
Look for hints that the writer may give you.

This Is the Idea

Read this weather report. Think about what will happen as time goes by.

The Week's Weather

Looking ahead, we see a warming trend. It's going to get warmer and warmer. Each day should be a little warmer than the last. By the end of the week, we may see a record high. Spring is really here.

You can predict that Tuesday will be warmer than Monday. You can also predict that Thursday will be even warmer. (Of course, weather forecasts are often wrong.)

Take a Closer Look

Read this recipe. Decide what will happen as the dish cooks.

What helps you
- what you know
- a pattern
- what the writer says will happen

An *Easy* Potato Dish

Peel and slice two potatoes. Peel and slice an onion. Spread the slices in a shallow baking pan. Pour chicken broth over the slices. Cover the pan tightly with foil. Bake for 20 minutes. The foil keeps the steaming broth inside, so the dish won't dry out as it cooks.

Circle your answers. *Hint:* Think about what the recipe says and what you know.

1. You bake the dish for five minutes. What will happen?
   a. It won't be cooked.   b. It will be overcooked.

2. You don't cover the pan. As time passes, what will happen?
   a. The dish will become moist.   b. The dish will dry out.

Try It

Read this health tip. Think about what happens as time passes.

 **BLOCK THAT SUN!** The sun warms you, but too much sunshine can hurt you. Some of the sun's rays harm your skin. The longer you stay in strong sunlight, the more harm those rays do. Stay too long, and your skin will burn. That's why you should limit your time in the summer sun.

Circle your answers.

1. What happens while you are in strong sunlight?
   a. The sun's rays harm your skin.
   b. The health tip doesn't say what happens.

2. You stay in strong sunlight for too long. What happens?
   a. The sun's rays don't harm your skin at all.
   b. Your skin burns.

Use It

Read this advice. Think about what will happen as you paint.

PAINTING SECRETS

When you paint a room, work from top to bottom. Why? No one can paint without a few spatters and drips. Suppose you paint the walls pink and then paint the ceiling white. You're sure to get some white polka dots on your nice pink walls.

Circle your answers.

1. You paint the walls green and then paint the ceiling yellow. What will probably happen?
   a. You will get some yellow spots on the green walls.
   b. You will get some green spots on the yellow ceiling.

2. You paint the ceiling tan and then paint the walls brown. What will probably happen?
   a. You will get some tan spots on the brown walls.
   b. You will cover any tan spots when you paint the walls.

Using Your Prediction

Lesson 25

♦ *Applying Predictions of Outcome*

Make your best guess about what may happen as time passes. (See Lesson 24.) Then plan what you should do.

This Is the Idea

Read this weather report. Think about what you should do.

> ### *This Week's Weather* _____
>
> Winter will arrive this week with snow and bitter cold. Snow will be light at the start of the week, but it will increase toward the end of the week. The days will be colder and colder as the week goes on.

As time passes, the days will get colder and colder. Snow will build up. What should you do? You'd better get those heavy coats and boots out of the back of the closet.

Take a Closer Look

Read this cooking tip. Think about what you should do as a cake bakes.

> Some ovens are hotter than others, even when they are at the same setting. If the heat is too high, a cake will bake too fast. When the baking time is up, the outside of the cake will be burned. Check your cake from time to time. It should bake evenly. If it's turning brown around the edges, then it's baking too fast.

Circle your answers.

1. What will happen if a cake bakes too fast?
   a. It won't be done. b. It will burn.

2. What should you do if your cake is turning brown around the edges? *Hint:* That means it's baking too fast.
   a. Turn the heat down. b. Turn the heat up.

Try It

Read this health tip. Think about what office workers should do.

GET UP AND *STRETCH!*

Many people work at desks all day long. If you're one of them, you may find that your back aches at the end of the day. You can avoid that. Keep track of time while you work. Every hour, get up and stretch. Walk around if you can. Even a very short break will help your back.

Circle your answers.

1. Keesha works at a desk all day long. What can you predict?
   a. Her back may ache.
   b. Her back will never ache.

2. What should Keesha do?
   a. Stay at her desk all day.
   b. Stretch every hour.

Use It

Read this public notice. Think about how to get to work.

BRIDGE CLOSING

The 12th Street Bridge will be closed for repairs next week. North Bridge will be for buses only that week. South Bridge will be the only way for cars to get into Center City. Extra subway trains and buses will be running that week.

Circle your answers.

1. What will probably happen at South Bridge next week?
   a. Traffic will be very light.
   b. Traffic will be very heavy.

2. What will probably happen if you try to drive your car over North Bridge next week?
   a. You will be stopped.
   b. You will have no trouble.

3. What will probably be the best way into Center City next week?
   a. Drive your car over the 12th Street Bridge.
   b. Take the bus or subway.

Thinking Clearly

◆ *Drawing Conclusions*

Statements work together. From one statement that makes sense, you can conclude, or figure out, that another statement makes sense.

This Is the Idea

Read this news report. What can you conclude about the events?

Flooding in Lincoln Square

CENTER CITY — A huge pipe burst below Lincoln Square. The square is now full of water. Police are keeping people out of Lincoln Square and the streets south of the square. Streets north of the square are open, but traffic will be heavy.

Suppose that you usually go through Lincoln Square to get to work. You can conclude that you'd better find another way.

Suppose that you usually go north of Lincoln Square to get to work. You can conclude that you'd better start early.

Take a Closer Look

This fact helps you know what makes sense

- What is true for a group is true for any thing in the group.

Read this notice. What can you conclude about who needs a shot?

FLU SHOTS

Who needs a flu shot? No one wants to get the flu, of course. But a case of the flu can be risky for people over 65. People with asthma or heart disease are at risk, too. So are women who are pregnant. Those people should get a flu shot in the fall. You may want to get one, too.

Aine is a healthy woman of 22. She is not pregnant. Daud is 72. He has had a heart attack. Which of them needs a flu shot more? Circle your answer. *Hint:* Decide which groups Aine and Daud belong in.

a. Aine   b. Daud

Try It

Read this article. What can you conclude about any penguin?

Penguins

Penguins are birds that cannot fly. Most penguins live in cold regions of the world. The King and Emperor penguins are the largest types. The smallest is the Little Blue penguin.
All penguins swim very well. They use their wings as paddles.

© Getty Images

Circle your answers.

1. What can you conclude about the Emperor penguin?
   a. It can fly.   b. It can't fly.

2. What can you conclude about the Little Blue penguin?
   a. It can swim.   b. It can't swim.

Use It

Read these job ads. What can you conclude about getting the jobs?

Trainee. Small midtown hotel. Earn while you learn. We will teach you hotel work. You don't have to have worked in a hotel before. Apply in person.

Desk Clerk. Small midtown hotel. Night shift. Must have worked as a desk clerk before. Must speak English and Spanish. Apply in person.

Circle your answers.

1. Delu doesn't mind working the night shift. She has never worked as a desk clerk before, but she thinks she would be good at it. Which job could she get?
   a. Trainee   b. Desk Clerk   c. either one

2. Cliff works as the night-time desk clerk at a large hotel. He'd like to move to a smaller one. He lived in Spain for years and speaks the language well. Which job could he get?
   a. Trainee   b. Desk Clerk   c. either one

3. Which job could you get?
   a. Trainee   b. Desk Clerk   c. either one

Using Clear Thinking

Think about what you can conclude from what you read. (See Lesson 26.) Then, think about what you should do.

This Is the Idea

Read this ad. What can you conclude about Saturday?

Family Day at Sunset Park

Calling all families! Next Saturday will be family day at Sunset Park. It will be a great day for kids of all ages. There will be special rides and games. There will be free snacks and hot dogs for kids. There will be clowns and a band. Adults can come, too. There will be fun for all.

You can conclude that there will be many children in Sunset Park on Saturday. What does that mean for you? If you have children, you may want to take them to the park that day. If you are looking for a quiet place to read and relax, you may want to stay away.

Take a Closer Look

Read this parents' guide. What can you conclude about the movie?

Space Pirates on Mars

Rated PG. Children under 6 may be frightened by this movie. They'll find the plot hard to follow, too. Children from 7 to 10 are sure to like it. It has enough action to hold their interest, and they'll get the jokes. Children 11 and older will find it too childish. It's not for them.

Suppose that you have two children. Zack is a boy of 9. Terri is a girl of 14. Which of them would you take to see *Space Pirates on Mars*? Circle your answer. *Hint:* Decide which groups Zack and Terri belong in.

a. Zack   b. Terri

Try It

Read this article. What can you conclude about the danger?

Good Weather Brings Fire Danger

We've had many warm, sunny days this fall. Our forests are very dry. The danger of fire is very high. A fire could start if a careless camper let a campfire get out of control. A fire could start if a smoker dropped a lighted match.

Circle your answers.

1. What can you conclude about building a campfire in the forest?
   a. It would be a good idea.
   b. It would be a bad idea.

2. You are planning a camping trip with friends. You love to sing songs around a campfire. What makes sense?
   a. Go later, when the forests are not so dry.
   b. Go now, because the weather is so nice.

Use It

Read about these courses. What can you conclude about them?

Child Care

Babies need love and lots of care. This course helps new parents help their children. Meets Tuesday and Thursday nights, weekly.

Home Repair

Learn how to fix leaky plumbing and other things around your home. Save money on repairs! Meets every Monday night.

Circle your answers.

1. For what reason would people take the home repair course?
   a. Something is broken.   b. They have new babies.

2. Who would you expect to meet at the child care course?
   a. plumbers   b. new parents

3. Sasha wants to take the home repair course. But he concludes that he can't. Why?
   a. He's a new parent.   b. He's busy on Monday nights.

Filling Gaps

Sometimes writers leave things out. They may even leave out their main point. As you read, make a good guess about what's missing.

This Is the Idea

Read this advice to home owners. Think about the writer's point.

Thawing Frozen Pipes

Always thaw frozen pipes the safe way. Use a hair dryer or heat lamp. These will warm pipes with no danger. Never use an open flame or boiling water. Those heat pipes too quickly and can make them explode.

The advice says that there are safe ways to thaw frozen pipes. Why would the writer say this? There must be ways that are not safe. You can infer that an open flame and boiling water are not safe. The advice doesn't say that, but you can guess.

Take a Closer Look

Read this column. Think about the writer's main point.

Getting a Pet? Be Prepared

Some people buy a dog at a pet shop and pay a lot of money. Others get a dog for free at an animal shelter. Both dogs will need shots each year. Those shots cost money. Both dogs will also eat food every day. That food can cost hundreds of dollars each year.

Which one of these is a good guess? Circle it. **Hints:** Look at what dogs need. Do those things cost money?

a. Even free dogs cost money.

b. Some dogs never cost their owners a cent.

Try It

Read this profile. Think about the writer's point.

A Hard-Working Writer

Isaac Asimov wrote every day. His work days were very long. He started work early each morning and wrote until late at night. He is best known for science fiction stories. He also wrote funny poems and books about history. All in all, he wrote more than 400 books.

Which of these are good guesses about Asimov? Check two.

_____ a. He was lazy.

_____ b. He loved to write.

_____ c. He had many interests.

_____ d. He was interested only in science.

Use It

Read this advice. Think about the writer's point.

Saving Money on Household Helpers

Many people use costly products in their homes. They buy mothballs, drain cleaners, and window cleaners. There are cheaper choices. Cedar chips can replace mothballs. Pouring boiling water down the kitchen drain once a week keeps it free of grease. Vinegar in water cleans windows.

Circle your answers.

1. Which sentence is a good guess?
   a. Cedar chips cost less than mothballs.
   b. Cedar chips cost more than mothballs.

2. Which sentence is a good guess?
   a. Boiling water costs less than drain cleaners.
   b. Boiling water costs more than drain cleaners.

3. Which sentence is a good guess?
   a. Window cleaners cost less than vinegar.
   b. Window cleaners cost more than vinegar.

Using Good Guesses

◆ *Applying Inferences*

As you read, make a good guess about what might be missing. (See Lesson 28.) Use your guess to plan what you should do.

This Is the Idea

Read this campaign ad. Think about the point of it.

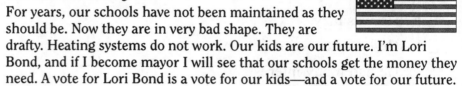

Bond for Mayor

For years, our schools have not been maintained as they should be. Now they are in very bad shape. They are drafty. Heating systems do not work. Our kids are our future. I'm Lori Bond, and if I become mayor I will see that our schools get the money they need. A vote for Lori Bond is a vote for our kids—and a vote for our future.

Lori Bond says that she will get the schools the money they need. What's missing? She doesn't say where that money will come from. Should you vote for her? First you may want to find out where she plans to get the money.

Take a Closer Look

Read this medicine label. Think about the writer's main point.

Cold-Be-Gone

Adults: Take one capful every four hours. Do not take more than four times a day.

Children over 5: Give no more than one capful per day. See your doctor if the cold lasts more than two days.

1. The point isn't stated. You have to guess it. Circle it.
   a. Cold-Be-Gone is safe no matter how much you take.
   b. Too much Cold-Be-Gone may be harmful.

2. Your little girl is 2. If she had a cold, what would you do? Circle your answer.
   a. Give her just a few drops of Cold-Be-Gone.
   b. Ask a doctor for advice.

Try It

Read this sports tip. Think about the writer's point.

Watching the Race

The Center City Foot Race will take place soon. Many people like to see the start. More like to see the finish. Those places are always crowded. Many people there can't see the race at all. But miles and miles along the course are not crowded.

Circle your answers.

1. Which of these is a good guess at the writer's point?
   a. The start and finish are the best places to watch the race.
   b. People can see the race better at other places on the course.

2. If you want to get a good view of the race, what should you do?
   a. Don't go to the start or finish.
   b. Go to the finish line.

Use It

Read this history article. Think about the writer's point.

Library of Congress, Prints & Photographs Division

Jane Addams and Hull House

In 1889 Jane Addams started Hull House in Chicago. She did it to help poor people. People who were new to the U.S. went there to learn to become citizens. Hull House began in one building. Today it fills many. All the money to run Hull House comes from people's gifts.

Circle your answers.

1. Which sentence is a good guess?
   a. Jane Addams was greedy.
   b. Jane Addams was generous.

2. Which sentence is a good guess?
   a. People's gifts of money have helped Hull House grow.
   b. Hull House has not done what Jane Addams wanted it to do.

3. For what reason would a person give money to Hull House?
   a. to move it out of Chicago
   b. to help needy families

Finding the Facts

Separating Fact from Opinion

**A *fact* is true.
An *opinion* is what
someone feels or
believes.
Different people
have different
feelings and beliefs.**

This Is the Idea

Read this part of a menu. Which parts could you prove?

Black Bean Soup ..... cup $1.00 ..... bowl $1.75

We make our soups fresh every day, and we use fresh ingredients.
This soup is made from black beans and vegetable broth.
It contains just five grams of fat but has nine grams of fiber.
It is a soothing and delicious treat on any cold day.

You could prove everything in black ink. You could watch the chef
make the soup. You could find out how to measure fat and fiber.
These are statements of fact.

You can't prove the statement in blue ink. That is the writer's
opinion. You may agree, or you may not.

Take a Closer Look

Statements of fact
- claim to be true
- can be checked

**Statements
of opinion**
- tell what
  someone feels
  or believes
- can't be checked

Read this column. Which parts are statements of fact?

Poor Families Face Housing Problems

In the U.S., many poor families are homeless or live in
shelters. Millions of others have homes. But many of those
homes are crowded and unsafe. They are awful places to live.
The people have to travel far to work or shop. These problems
should not exist in such a rich country.

Underline the statements of fact. *Hints:* Read each sentence. Ask
yourself if there is some way that you could prove it.

Two statements are not facts. Draw a line though them. *Hint:* Look
for statements that tell what the writer feels or believes.

Try It

Read this review of a play. Which parts are statements of fact?

HUSHED VOICES

reviewed by Leah Fitch ———————————————————
The play opens with a bare stage and dim lights. The walls are completely gray. The actors are also wearing gray or black. One by one, they step forward and speak. It is a boring start to an even more boring play. After the first act, I needed a breath of fresh air.

Put a check mark in front of each statement of fact. You can test a statement of fact. You can prove that a fact is true.

_____ a. The play opens with a bare stage and dim lights.

_____ b. The walls are completely gray.

_____ c. The actors are also wearing gray or black.

_____ d. It is a boring start to an even more boring play.

Use It

Read this part of an article. Which parts are statements of fact?

The Quill Pig

The porcupine is an odd-looking animal. For years, it was called a quill pig. It does look a bit like a pig, and it does have quills. Quills are the stiff, sharp spikes that cover its body. The quills have small barbs on them, like fish hooks. Those barbs are nasty!

© Getty Images

Put a check mark in front of each statement of fact. You can test a statement of fact. You can prove that a fact is true.

_____ a. The porcupine is an odd-looking animal.

_____ b. For years, it was called a quill pig.

_____ c. Quills are the stiff, sharp spikes that cover its body.

_____ d. The quills have small barbs on them, like fish hooks.

_____ e. Those barbs are nasty!

Thinking about Opinions

◆ *Evaluating Opinions*

An *opinion* is what someone feels or believes. Reasons should support them. Facts should back them up. Look for reasons and facts before agreeing with an opinion.

This Is the Idea

Read this news report. Look for facts and opinions.

New Highway Planned

CENTER CITY — The mayor of Center City said that the city will build a new highway. It will run beside Clear Lake. Clear Lake is in the heart of the city. There is no road beside the lake now. The land is not being used now.

There are no opinions in the news report. Every sentence states a fact. Those statements could be checked.

As you read, look for

- reasons for an opinion
- facts that back up an opinion

Take a Closer Look

Read this part of a speech. Think about the mayor's opinion.

From the Mayor's Speech

"Center City needs this highway. Downtown traffic is heavy. It has never been so heavy. To get through the city, trucks have to go on local streets. They crowd the streets. The new highway will get the trucks off our streets. That's why we need it."

Circle your answers.

1. What does the mayor think the city needs?
   a. a new highway   b. more trucks

2. Does the mayor state reasons and facts? *Hint:* Look for statements that tell why a highway would help. Look for statements that could be checked.
   a. yes   b. no

Try It

Read this column. Think about the writer's opinion.

DON'T SPOIL CLEAR LAKE, PLEASE

We do need a new highway. But it should not be beside Clear Lake. A park would be a better use of that land. The city has no downtown parks now. There is land for a highway outside the city. Building the highway there would cost less than building it in the city.

Circle your answers.

1. What does the writer think the city needs?
   a. a new highway beside Clear Lake and a park outside the city
   b. a new highway outside the city and a park beside Clear Lake

2. Which sentence states a fact to back up the writer's opinion?
   a. A park would be a better use of that land.
   b. The city has no downtown parks now.

Use It

Read this letter. Think about the writer's opinion.

To the Editor:

Both plans for the Clear Lake land are foolish. Parks are a waste of land. Highways are ugly. Business is the best use of city land. We should sell the land to the highest bidder.

Edward Drake

Circle your answers.

1. What does Edward Drake think the city should do?
   a. Leave the land beside Clear Lake as it is now.
   b. Use the land for a highway.
   c. Sell the land for as much as it can get.

2. How many sentences in the letter state facts?
   a. none
   b. one
   c. three

Answer Key

Lesson 1

Take a Closer Look
1. c 2. b 3. c 4. a

Try It
1. a 2. b 3. a 4. b 5. a

Use It
1. a 2. a 3. b 4. b 5. b

Lesson 2

Take a Closer Look
1. b 2. a 3. c

Try It
Answers will vary.

Use It
Answers will vary.

Lesson 3

Take a Closer Look
1. a 2. a

Try It
1. a 2. b

Use It
1. b 2. a 3. b 4. a

Lesson 4

Take a Closer Look
earphones, volume, music

Try It
Answers will vary. Words should relate to using a phone, such as *dial*, *call*, *recall*, and *send*.

Use It
1. b 2. b 3. a

Lesson 5

Take a Closer Look
a, c

Try It
b, c

Use It
b, c, d, e, f

Lesson 6

Take a Closer Look
a, c

Try It
1. a 2. b

Use It
1. a 2. b 3. a 4. b

Lesson 7

Take a Closer Look
1. a 2. a

Try It
1. Put under "What I Know."
2. Put under "What I Want to Know."
3. Answers will vary. Put under "What I Know."
4. Answers will vary. Put under "What I Want to Know."

Use It
Answers will vary. Put under "What I Learned."

Lesson 8

Take a Closer Look
b

Try It
a, c

Use It
b

Lesson 9

Take a Closer Look
1. b   2. a

Try It
1. b   2. b   3. a

Use It
1. a   2. b   3. b

Lesson 10

Take a Closer Look
b, c

Try It
b, c

Use It
1. b   2. b   3. b

Lesson 11

Take a Closer Look
1. b

2. You should see your dentist twice a year for an exam.

Try It
1. a   2. a

Use It
1. b   2. a

Lesson 12

Take a Closer Look
b, c

Try It
c, d

Use It
1. b   2. b, c

Lesson 13

Take a Closer Look
b, c

Try It
b, c, d

Use It
d, e, f, g

Lesson 14

Take a Closer Look
a, d

Try It
a, c, d

Use It
1. b   2. a, b

Lesson 15

Take a Closer Look
a

Try It
3, 2, 5, 4, 1

Use It
4, 3, 1, 5, 2

Lesson 16

Take a Closer Look
1. b   2. a

Try It
1. a   2. a

Use It
1. b   2. b

Lesson 17

Take a Closer Look
1. b   2. b

Try It
1. a   2. a

Use It
1. b   2. a   3. b

Lesson 18

Take a Closer Look
1. a   2. a

Try It
1. b   2. b

Use It
1. b   2. c

Lesson 19

Take a Closer Look
1. d   2. b

Try It
1. a   2. b

Use It
1. b   2. b   3. c

Lesson 20

Take a Closer Look
1. b   2. b

Try It
1. c   2. b

Use It
1. a   2. c   3. b

Lesson 21

Take a Closer Look
a, b

Try It
b, c

Use It
b, c, d, e

Lesson 22

Take a Closer Look
b, c

Try It
a, c

Use It
a, e, f

Lesson 23

Take a Closer Look
1. b   2. b

Try It
1. a   2. b

Use It
1. b   2. b

Lesson 24

Take a Closer Look
1. a   2. b

Try It
1. a   2. b

Use It
1. a   2. b

Lesson 25

Take a Closer Look
1. b   2. a

Try It
1. a   2. b

Use It
1. b   2. a   3. b

Lesson 26

Take a Closer Look
b

Try It
1. b   2. a

Use It
1. a

2. c

3. Answers will vary.

Lesson 27

Take a Closer Look
a

Try It
1. b   2. a

Use It
1. a   2. b   3. b

Lesson 28

Take a Closer Look
a

Try It
b, c

Use It
1. a   2. a   3. b

Lesson 29

Take a Closer Look
1. b   2. b

Try It
1. b   2. a

Use It
1. b   2. a   3. b

Lesson 30

Take a Closer Look
Statements of fact—should be underlined:
In the U.S., many poor families are homeless or live in shelters.
Millions of others have homes.
But many of those homes are crowded and unsafe.
The people have to travel far to work or shop.

Statements of opinion—should be crossed out:
They are awful places to live.
These problems should not exist in such a rich country.

Try It
a, b, c

Use It
b, c, d

Lesson 31

Take a Closer Look
1. a   2. a

Try It
1. b   2. b

Use It
1. c   2. a